to C

Bon appetit

Rudolph Stanish

W9-AGF-621

OMELETS, CRÊPES, AND OTHER RECIPES

RUDOLPH STANISH

NEW YORK, NEW YORK

1970

COPYRIGHT © 1970 BY RUDOLPH STANISH

Library of Congress Catalog Card Number: 75–136752

HARBOR PRESS, INC., NEW YORK

"Une omelette est a la cuisine ce que le sonnet est a la poesie"

An omelet is to cooking what a sonnet is to poetry. Thus Alexander Dumas, great French dramatist and novelist, gourmet and amateur cook, wrote of this great French invention and he should have added that, like the soufflé, this *bouchée* of edible poetry does not wait for you, you wait for it.

TO MRS. PAUL MELLON
OAK SPRINGS, UPPERVILLE, VIRGINIA

PREFACE

FOR MANY YEARS I have been storing up ideas for my cook book, and many friends and clients keep asking for a book on household hints, recipes, and how to entertain. In this book you will find ways to keep your pots and pans shining like those of Mrs. Richard Rodgers, including recipes I have been using for years in the homes of my clients all over the country. Many are first-hand from the kitchen of Mrs. Thomas B. Hess, always encouraging and sharing with me her vast collection of unusual recipes. A bigger book will come later . . . I have taken the advice of Mrs. Paul Mellon, who said, "Stanish, write it as you would say it."

THE CONTENTS

INTRODUCTION

HISTORY OF COOKING

Isn't it exciting and fun to imagine what life must have been like in Prehistoric times? The principal occupation of the head of the family had to be the hunter-provider. In the beginning he probably had to be the cook too, as only he could manage the fire, from starting it—to tending it—to cooking the food. No cooking utensils were used then, and food was cooked in the hot ashes. However, man soon discovered that flat rocks and stones could be heated and food cooked on them. Then someone discovered that hollows in the rocks where water could be held, could be used to make broth or soup by dropping hot stones in the mixture of water and food.

Eventually early man found that grilling food over an open fire improved the flavor. Then he designed the spit and cooked food by suspending and turning it over the hot coals. By now man had overcome his fear of the flames and fire, and it became a part of the family's daily life. The cooking job was gradually given to the woman in the family. The job of turning the spit was usually entrusted to the eldest son.

Years later, after man learned more about the control of fire, it went into the home, and the fireplace became the center of family activities. It was the source of heating as well as cooking. Then women took over most of the cooking job. In the early 1500's a big black iron pot or caldron was the only cooking utensil. Everything was cooked in it. Finally, when the stove was invented, more and more of the iron pots, caldrons of every size, soup kettles, kitchen tools, and tableware appeared.

Today some of the old black coal or wood stoves of our most recent ancestors are collectors' items, and they are used for decor. One manufacturer has even taken a coal stove and modernized it with gas units. For the most part, however, coal stoves have all been replaced in today's homes with gas or electric ranges of steel, chrome and enamel. Instead of striking a match, you now push a button, or turn a control knob, to get any degree of heat you need for cooking.

Most important in today's world of fashion and style, cooking utensils have changed into beautiful, colorful pieces of equipment that are decorative as well as useful. They can be chosen in designs and colors to match or accent any color scheme; and to make your kitchen as much of a "show place" as any other room in your home.

SOME INCOMPLETE THOUGHTS ON COOKING

The answer to the often-asked question—what makes a good cook?—depends on how well one can judge a good cook.

Like fingerprints, no two cooks are alike.

A good cook must always be self-critical and never lose his love of experimentation.

If one plans to make cooking a life work one must love the art.

Of course, like a ballet dancer, a cook should start early in life, but I have known many who developed the art later in life. I think the *love* of cooking often can make the difference between a dub and an expert.

All people should *know* about food, if for no other reason than the pleasure involved.

Start simple and when confidence is attained, have the courage to try your wings on more complicated dishes. If you have a Fanny Farmer cookbook, you're in business.

Save your menus no matter how simple the meal. Later on they will not only show your development, but will remind you of past triumphs you can produce again.

Strive to please whom you are cooking for. Besides *your* pride of accomplishment, *their* pleasure is much of your satisfaction and reward.

FOR BEST COOKING RESULTS

In CLUB ALUMINUM most cooking can be done over LOW heat.

That's because aluminum s-p-r-e-a-d-s heat (any fuel) rapidly, way beyond the burner flame. The heat travels swiftly across the bottom and up the sides, spreading it through the whole utensil. This fast, even-spreading of heat makes possible creamy white sauces that stay white; cooks all foods gently, perfectly; and keeps roasts juicier. In baking, it produces more uniform texture and brownness.

Aluminum utensils are light to handle, reducing fatigue—yet are strong, sturdy and last practically forever.

Aluminum is known as the "friendly-to-food" metal.

Here's Why: Aluminum is the most abundant of all elements in the earth's crust. Practically all growing things absorb small amounts of natural aluminum. It is even found in most of the foods we eat.

Scientists know that aluminum cannot impart any taste or color, or anything else, to foods cooked in it. In fact, the purity of distilled water is protected in aluminum.

Aluminum utensils are used in the overwhelming majority of all hospitals and in food manufacturing plants. You'll find, too, that delicate foods, such as cheese, butter and candy are protected in aluminum foil.

ALUMINUM UTENSILS ARE READY FOR USE— NEED NO SEASONING

All CLUB ALUMINUM utensils—even fry pans, dutch ovens, griddles and the like—require no special "seasoning." They are ready for use after being washed in hot, soapy water to remove any manufacturing film or dust that may have accumulated.

Just pull off label and wash off adhesive with warm water. If label sticks, moisten with water or cover with damp cloth. *Do not scrape*, lest you mar the highly polished surface.

IT'S EASY TO KEEP ALUMINUM GLEAMING

Aluminum cooking utensils are easy to keep beautiful with this simple care:

1. After each use, wash aluminum utensils in hot, sudsy water and rinse in clear water and dry.

2. Don't leave an aluminum utensil partially immersed in a dishpan. This may darken it. Washing pots and pans in a dishwasher is not generally recommended. Some detergents, combined with local waters may discolor any metal utensil. Colored aluminum may fade in a dishwasher.

3. Steel wool and soap pads usually remove dried-on foods and grease quickly. If not, fill pan with warm water and let soak for 5–10 minutes; then scrape with a wooden spoon. (A knife or other metal may scratch the pan.)

4. Occasional polishing with silver polish renews the bright finish on the outside.

KEEP ALUMINUM BRIGHT

With the simple care, as given above, aluminum utensils will last for practically a lifetime. They're ideal for every cooking use, and daily cleaning with steel wool or soap pads is recommended to keep grease and stains from accumulating. For top range cooking, low heat gives best results and prevents foods from burning and sticking.

Certain foods and waters sometimes cause discoloration on the inside of aluminum utensils. This is merely a harmless mineral deposit and forms much as tarnish does on silver.

These absolutely harmless stains are easily removed with steel wool and soap pads. Or, 2 tablespoons of cream of tartar in a quart of water, boiled in the pan for about 10 minutes, will brighten the inside.

Sometimes after using an aluminum pan for a while small marks or pits may appear in the bottom. This is caused by tiny quantities of mineral salts that may come from water or highly seasoned foods left standing in the pan. These pits do not hurt the pan, nor do they affect the food. Daily scouring, washing without soaking, helps prevent them.

Often a harmless lime deposit forms when water is left standing in a teakettle. This can be lessened if the kettle is emptied each night and dried for a minute over low heat. These deposits can sometimes be removed by placing the empty kettle over low heat until the lime dries and cracks. Tap bottom with wooden spoon to loosen the coating.

In some cases, a light coating of lime can be removed by boiling a strong solution of vinegar in the kettle for about 10 minutes; then rinse and dry.

Too much heat, or sudden temperature changes, such as pouring cold water into a hot empty pan, cause bottoms to warp.

[4]

A warped bottom on a sheet or stamped aluminum utensil can be easily fixed. If the pan bulges outward, place it bottom up on a smooth surface. Lay a flat piece of wood across the bottom and pound the wood gently down with a hammer. If the warped bottom bulges inward, set the pan right side up on a flat surface. Place a piece of wood inside the pan and pound gently down.

THE FEATURES TO LOOK FOR IN SELECTING COOKWARE

For even and quick cooking be sure the material from which your cookware is made is a good heat conductor. Some metals and ceramic materials used for cookware do not conduct heat evenly and quickly, and unless heat is carefully controlled food will stick and burn. When this happens, you usually end up with a ruined meal and a pan that is difficult to clean. So consider the type of material in your utensils, as well as the appearance.

Flat unpolished bottoms will give you a good heat absorbing surface. The flat bottom is also designed to make the best contact with your source of heat. Incidentally, the circled bottoms on some utensils give excellent heat conductivity on both gas and electric heating units.

Bright or shiny finishes reflect heat and should not be used on the bottom of cooking utensils.

Straight or slightly tapered sides with rounded contours at the bottom make cookware easier to clean. Straight sides also enable the pan to properly cover the burner. The rounded corners make it easier for stirring, and turning too.

Utensils without rolled edges, rivets, or seams are easier to keep clean. Rimless top edges will also make pouring easier. If you prefer a utensil with a rolled edge be sure it is turned and rolled to form a flat rim or bead on top so a cover will fit properly. Also make sure the seam under the edge is tight to the body of the pan, so food and moisture cannot collect.

Whatever the material you select it should be safe, easy to clean, and durable enough to withstand normal household use. Take your time and be selective about choosing your cookware. Buy the best quality you can afford as in the long run it will be less expensive and will give you better service as well as cooking satisfaction.

[5]

THE COVER STORY

One part of every top stove utensil that is of major importance is the cover. You can tell a good utensil by the cover. Sturdy, durable, properly fitting covers are essential if you want to become a good cook.

Look for the heavier, solid covers which will not quiver or wobble when cooking. These are the kind of covers which will help you retain the maximum flavors and food value nature put in food. The best covers are as heavy as the pan itself and they should both fit well and have a flange to seal in all the juices and moisture. When moisture is held in the pan, food is cooked in its own natural juices and basted again and again.

Cover knobs should be sturdy, easily grasped, securely attached, and made of heat resistant material. Check the handles and knobs by lifting the pan, the cover, and then both together. Make sure they are easy to grasp and easy to hold. This will save burned fingers.

Select the style, finish, and color you want for your kitchen. If you will use care and good judgment in choosing the design best for your needs, and watch your covers, you cannot help but build a well planned set of cookware.

I

Omelets

EGG NUTRITIVE VALUE

Eggs are recommended by nutritionists and medical authorities to be included in the diet in some form every day. The protein in eggs is complete, furnishing all of the amino acids essential for building and maintaining body tissues.

Eggs contain vitamin A, the B vitamins—thiamine, riboflavin and niacin—and vitamin D, plus the essential minerals, iron and phosphorus.

Two eggs weighing 2 ounces each furnish 17% of an adult's recommended daily protein allowance, yet have only 77 calories per egg.

EGG QUALITY AND GRADING

The federal grading designations for eggs are AA, A, B and C. Grades AA and A are high quality eggs with large proportions of thick white which stands up well around a firm, high yolk—especially desirable for poaching, hardcooking in the shell and frying. In B and C grade eggs the white is thinner and the yolk flattened. These eggs are suitable for use in scrambling, baking and general cooking. The air cell in a high quality egg should be very small.

Very infrequently, blood spots appear in eggs. They may be lifted out before cooking and do not alter nutritive value, cooking performance, or taste of the egg.

EGG SIZE

The size of eggs is based on minimum weight per dozen. The sizes are Jumbo (30 oz.), Extra Large (27 oz.), Large (24 oz.), Medium (21 oz.) and Small (18 oz.). Some homemakers prefer the larger eggs for use at breakfast and for main dishes at luncheon

[7]

and dinner. Medium or Small eggs are often preferred for deviled eggs and lunch box or picnic foods.

EGG COLOR

The color of the egg shell may vary from white to deep brown. Shell color has no effect on the food value, flavor or quality of the egg.

DID YOU KNOW ...

1. Eggs are included in one of the four food groups of the popular Daily Food Guide planned by the U.S. Department of Agriculture. The group also includes poultrymeats, fish, and meat. Other groups are: dairy foods, fruits and vegetables, and bread and cereals.

2. Eggs are important in reducing diets. They contain generous amounts of protein and other essential nutrients with a modest number of calories—154 in a 2-egg serving.

3. Eggs are an excellent source of the highest quality complete protein, containing all of the essential amino acids.

4. Cooked egg yolk is one of the first solid foods fed to babies.

5. Depending on the size 4 to 6 whole eggs, 6 to 10 egg whites, or 12 to 19 egg yolks are equivalent to 1 standard measuring cup.

6. For a quick, thorough separation of yolks from whites, bring eggs to room temperature. (Remove eggs from refrigerator about 45 minutes before separating.)

7. Eggs beat up faster and to larger volume when brought to room temperature.

8. In combining hot mixtures and eggs as in custards, cream fillings, souffles, etc., the hot mixture should be poured slowly into the beaten egg, stirring or beating constantly.

9. Leftover egg yolks may be hard cooked and used in salads, and sandwiches, and scalloped dishes.

10. Many authorities believe that eggs and chickens reached the Western Hemisphere with the second voyage of Columbus in 1493.

ABOUT THE EGG INDUSTRY

From the pin-money operation of a few generations ago, the egg industry has progressed to today's giant enterprise, returning about two billion dollars annually to the American farmer. It represents his third largest source of income, exceeded only by livestock production and dairy farming.

Research has brought about our modern methods of egg production and marketing. Greater efficiency and know-how in operation take eggs from the farm to the family table and assure today's consumer of a top quality product. Packed with essential nutrients, eggs are one of our most nearly perfect foods.

HOW TO BUY AND STORE EGGS WISELY

Two factors that affect the price of eggs are grade and size. When buying eggs, consider the grade (or quality) best suited to the intended use.

The care of eggs in the home is important to protecting the quality.

Remember these points:

1. Keep in the refrigerator.

2. Store with the large end up.

3. Remove from the refrigerator only the number needed at one time.

4. Leftover egg whites may be held a week to ten days if they are stored in the refrigerator in a tightly covered container.

5. Store leftover yolks *under water* in a covered container in the refrigerator. They may be held 2 to 3 days.

THE RIGHT PAN

A special pan should be kept solely for making omelets and crêpes. It should be of cast aluminum. Its sides should be sloping and it should measure 8 to 10 inches across. Weight can vary according to preference. I use the CLUB ALUMINUM omelet pan of heavy cast aluminum. The omelet pan should have rounded sloping shoulders which allows the egg mixture to spread and, when tilted, to slide easily onto the plate when cooked. Ideally, the omelet pan should measure 7 inches in diameter, be made of heavy cast aluminum or iron with a long sturdy handle. The same pan can be used for making crêpe (page 29). All cooks are agreed the omelet pan should be kept exclusively for making omelets, so one should not be tempted to use it for other cooking, with the exception of crêpes. After use, it should be wiped carefully and thoroughly with paper towelling and put away against the next time omelets are in order.

The pan should never be washed in a detergent. To clean away small egg particles that may remain, use a little salt and wipe out with a paper towel. If a cast aluminum pan is selected, polish the inside surface with a soaped steel wool pad till shiny. The pan should never be washed again.

When using a new pan, be generous with the butter. The more the pan is used, the better it becomes. If you get in trouble and some day an omelet sticks, clean the pan by scouring it with salt and wipe it out with a paper towel. Or shine occasionally with a soap brillo pad.

SOME IMPORTANT POINTS

1. Always use salted butter.

2. Keep pan on a medium heat with the heat readily adjustable.

3. Have ingredients and things to be added readily available.

4. Banish everything but the care of the omelet from your mind, and concentrate on the eggs.

5. Serve the omelet immediately.

In most cases leftover vegetables, rice, or seafoods marry to perfection embraced with pure egg and rolled into a voluptuous omelet. It has been proven many times in our daily dining that food tastes better when given the second heat. Vegetables really come to life with a sprinkle of cheese before rolling the omelet. It then should be left to sit one moment before eating. Most vegetables are moist so they should be left to drain before adding them to the egg. But foods other than leftovers work just as well —from fresh herbs to caviar.

All omelet fillings should be very fine in texture (by chopping or whatever) before filling. Do not skimp when making the sauce —when a sauce is called for.

THE PERFECT OMELET IS NOTHING BUT SKILL

Being able to make a perfect omelet is as necessary to the good life as making a good cup of coffee or tea. But a perfect omelet has the advantage of changing its character to fit all types of menu planning and social life.

The omelet can be a main course dish, a dessert, a feature at a cocktail party or at a reception. It can be all things to all people and all occasions. The only requirement is that it be a perfect specimen of omelet cookery. And that takes nothing but skill, which means attention to details.

A perfect omelet is pure gold, never brown, light and delicate in texture, soft and voluptuous in the center. In addition to fresh eggs and the best-quality butter, the other ingredients in making a splendid omelet are practice—there is no substitute for this— the right pan and a generous dash of self confidence.

A few simple rules in the preparation and presentation of omelets:

- Eggs should be at room temperature. Allow an hour after they come from the refrigerator.

- Care should be taken *not* to overbeat the eggs or they will become thin and the omelet will be tough.

- Butter should always be used but never allowed to brown before adding the omelet mixture. Otherwise, it will change the color but, further, may make the omelet stick.

- Omelets should always be served at once on warm, not hot, plates or they will go on cooking.

The omelet is not only economical but extremely versatile. The basic omelet with a simple green garnish, crusty bread and a glass of chilled, dry white wine, is elegant enough to serve to the most sophisticated palate, but the omelet can be used to embrace other ingredients—seafood, vegetables, poultry, cheese, sweetbreads, chicken livers, certain purées, even certain leftovers—to become a truly luxurious dish. Once you have mastered this *art de la cuisine*, give your imagination free reign and serve omelets as the main dish, as a dessert, and as a real dazzler at your parties.

OMELET RECIPES

These recipes for omelets are the ones most in demand for luncheons and suppers. There are many more, however, and I will just mention a few of the different meats and vegetables that can be mixed into the beaten eggs.

It is to be remembered that once your aluminum omelet pan has been seasoned that only two foods may go into the pan with the butter. These are herbs and bacon which has been rendered of its fat. All other foodstuffs are mixed into the eggs.

One exception is cheese, which may be spread or sprinkled on top of the eggs just before rolling the omelet onto a dish.

These are some foods and the amounts to add to a two- or three-egg omelet:

1. *Truffles*—Dice one truffle and let stand in 1 tablespoon of heavy cream while you prepare the eggs. Over this omelet sprinkle a teaspoon of fines herbes.

2. *Anchovies*—Take one rolled or two strips of anchovy and rub through a sieve. Mix with 2 teaspoons water. Add to egg mixture as you beat the eggs.

3. *Brussel Sprouts*—Dice two or three sprouts that have been cooked and add to the egg mixture with 1 teaspoon of fines herbes.

4. *Baby Peas and Cottage Cheese*—Add one tablespoon each of cooked peas and small-curd cottage cheese into the eggs.

5. *Cauliflower*—Dice fine one or two rosettes of cooked cauliflower, fry in butter until slightly brown and add to eggs.

6. *Fines Herbes*—This omelet should be made with one good tablespoon of the herbs and two spring onions, diced fine. Sauté all in butter and then add to beaten eggs. It should appear quite green.

[12]

7. *Spinach*—Moisten one heaping tablespoon of left-over spinach (chopped) with one tablespoon of heavy cream and add a little pinch of fresh nutmeg gratings. Add this into the beaten eggs.

8. *Potato and Onion*—Dice one small onion and one potato. Sauté in a little cooking oil, the potato first and then the onion. Add ½ teaspoon paprika. When cool add to the beaten eggs.

9. *Meats, Fish, Chicken, etc.*—Sprinkle a little fines herbes into the buttered pan. Add one tablespoon of leftover diced chicken, shrimp, ham, lobster or veal to the beaten eggs. Any of these make a tasty omelet.

How to saute mushrooms the professional way: Heat a large, heavy skillet (not cast iron because it discolors mushrooms). Add enough butter or butter and vegetable oil (half and half) to coat the surface of the pan generously. When very hot, but not brown, add the mushrooms, whole, sliced or chopped (whatever the recipe calls for). Spread over the entire surface of the pan. As soon as the edges begin to turn brown, turn and brown lightly on the other side. Takes about 4 minutes. Lift out of skillet and drain on paper towels.

The easy way to sauté chopped or sliced onions: Melt butter in a heavy saucepan just large enough to accommodate the amount of onion called for comfortably. Add ½ cup of water, about, place pan over a high heat and bring up to a boil. Boil over moderate heat until all the water has evaporated and onions are cooked, but not brown, and only butter is left. If water boils away and onions are not tender, add more water and continue cooking.

How to peel and seed tomatoes: Drop firm, ripe tomatoes into boiling water to cover. Allow to stand briefly or actually boil for 10 seconds. Cut out the stems, peel off the skin, starting from the stem end. Cut in half (peeled or unpeeled) cross wise, and squeeze each half gently to extract the seeds from the center.

How to make a bouquet of herbs: The basis of fine herbs should be parsley. If properly made, it can be stored in a jar and refrigerated and should last a week. Wash the herbs in cold water, shake off excess moisture. Trim and discard the stems off a bunch of parsley. Chop parsley coarse, enough to fill a cup. Take a bunch of fresh chives and cut fine. Enough to make 3 tablespoonfuls and add 2 blades of fresh tarragon and about a tablespoonful of the leaves of fresh dill. Now chop all this together very fine. Place on a cloth and roll up and wring out all the moisture. Place in a jar and store in refrigerator.

THE PLAIN BASIC OMELET

An omelet for one person, as a main dish, calls for:

    3 eggs*
    1 tablespoon cold water
    4 drops Tabasco, about
    ¼ teaspoon salt, scant
    1 tablespoon lightly-salted butter

Beat eggs with a rotary beater or whisk until they begin to foam. Take care not to overbeat or they will become liquid, like water. Properly beaten, they look "stringy" and make threads when you lift up the beater or whisk.

Heat the pan over medium heat until hot. To test, flick a few drops of water on the pan. If it jumps around, your pan is ready; if steam rises, the pan is too hot. In which case, take off the heat and wave in the air to cool it down. Add the butter (*if it's a new pan*, butter the sides all the way up to the top).

Pour the eggs into the hot pan. Then with the flat side of a fork, make circular motions around the bottom of the pan *fast*, as you would making scrambled eggs. Speed is of the essence for lightness and fluffiness. While the right hand makes a circular motion, shake the pan with the left hand, rocking it back and forth, to keep the eggs loose. When the eggs are cooked and all the liquid is firm, spread the eggs evenly, but lightly, with a fork to cover any breaks in the surface. Pause briefly to allow the eggs to set.

To turn the omelet out, grasp the handle of the pan with your left hand, *palm side up* (this makes it easier to tilt the pan and finally roll the omelet out). Now tilt the pan at a 45° angle and, with the fork in your right hand, as close as possible to the handle, begin to roll the omelet away from the handle to the opposite edge of the pan and onto a heated plate.

The perfect omelet is firm on the outside, pure egg color without any brown, fluffy and soufflé-like on the inside.

With practice, any cook can, and should, do the entire operation in 1 minute flat and the omelet should be served at once.

* In making several or many omelets, it is useful to have a half-cup dipper with a long handle to measure the quantity for each omelet exactly.

Note: Omelets, unlike other egg cookery which is always slow, are cooked fast over high heat.

OMELET PARTY FOR 12

When you give an omelet party, it is attractive to offer a variety of garnishes so that each guest can choose what he likes best. The recipe for, and the cooking of, the basic omelet remains the same.

In a 2-quart bowl, have combined and ready to use:

> 2 dozen eggs
> ¼ cup cold water
> ½ teaspoon Tabasco
> 1 teaspoon salt

On the counter, near the range:

> ¼ pound (1 stick) lightly-salted butter, unwrapped,
>   sliced into 12 tablespoons
> 1 heated omelet pan on the heat (low)
> 1 stack heated plates (12)
> ½ cup ladle

At hand, these garnishes, each in a separate bowl:

> ½ cup finely-chopped fresh parsley, chives, and
>   tarragon or basil, mixed
> 1 pound bacon, cooked and crumbled
> ½ pound Parmesan, Swiss or Cheddar cheese,
>   freshly grated
> 1 pound chopped and sautéed mushrooms

[15]

Grease sides and bottom with one table-spoon butter. Pan is hot enough when a few drops of water jump and disappear. If pan is too hot, wave in air to cool.

For a standard-size omelet use ⅔ cup beaten eggs, which is about 3 eggs. For a small reception omelet, suitable for cock-tail parties, use ⅓ cup.

Working fast, make quick circular motions with a fork flat on bottom of pan. Shake pan to and fro while stirring. All this is to raise layers of fluffiness.

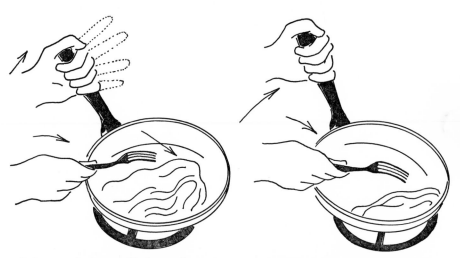

Before you begin to roll, change the position of your hand on handle to palm-side up, making it easier to tilt pan so that gravity will assist in the rolling.

At all times in the rolling, use the fork lightly and delicately — never pressing, only lifting. Object is to preserve fluffiness already achieved by fast stirring.

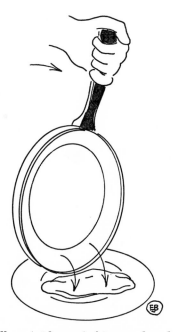

Roll out (without a fork) onto a hot plate. Inside of omelet goes on cooking, so place on plate when about 95 per cent done. Total process takes one minute plus.

Illustrations by James Edward Brown

OMELET GRAND'MÈRE

        3 slices bacon
        Basic Omelet Recipe for 1 [page 14]
        1 tablespoon finely chopped parsley, chives, mixed,
            and a leaf of tarragon, [if available]
        1 tablespoon freshly grated Parmesan or Swiss

Pile the bacon slices on top of each other, then, using a good sharp knife, cut across them about 20 times. Place in a cold pan, over moderate heat, and fry until brown. Drain on paper towelling.

Have the omelet pan heated with the butter, *for one omelet*, add the herb mixture and cook 1 minute. Add the bacon bits, then the egg mixture. Follow cooking instructions for Basic Omelet (page 00).

When omelet is set, sprinkle with the cheese, roll out onto a heated plate and serve at once. Serves 1.

RED CAVIAR AND SOUR CREAM OMELET

        1 tablespoon red caviar
        2 tablespoons sour cream
        1 heaping teaspoon freshly minced herbs
        Basic Omelet Recipe for 1 [page 14]

Mix the caviar into the sour cream. Have the omelet mixture ready and the pan on the heat. Add the butter, *for one omelet*, to the pan and *1 level teaspoon of the herbs*. Cook for 1 minute. Add the eggs and finish the omelet. Once the omelet is on the serving plate, make a slit down the center and spoon in the caviar mixture. Sprinkle with the remaining herbs and serve immediately. Delicious with a glass of chilled champagne.

OMELET WITH CHICKEN LIVER GARNISH

        ½ pound fresh chicken livers
        2 tablespoons butter
        2 tablespoons dry sherry
        Big pinch arrowroot
        Basic Omelet Recipe for 1 [page 14]
        2 teaspoons fresh mixed herbs (parsley, chives and
            tarragon or basil), chopped fine

If the gall has not been removed from the livers, as it should be, cut it off. Then slice each liver across 3 times. In a medium saucepan, heat the butter. When it just begins to turn brown, add the livers and sauté quickly over a high heat until delicately colored all over. About 1 minute. Heat the sherry, ignite, and pour flaming over the livers. Take the pan off the heat, sprinkle the arrowroot over all, then stir into the liquid to thicken lightly. Cover. Set aside and keep warm.

Have the omelet mixture ready and the pan on the heat. Add the butter, *for one omelet,* to the pan, and *1 teaspoon of the fresh herb mixture.* Cook 1 minute. Add the eggs and finish the omelet. Once the omelet is on the serving plate, make a slit down the top with a small sharp knife, almost the entire length. Spoon 3 tablespoons of the liver garnish into the opening. Serve with a few sprigs of fresh watercress. Make a second omelet using the remainder of the liver garnish.

SAUERKRAUT AND SAUSAGE OMELET

    4 breakfast sausages
    1 16-ounce can of sauerkraut, well drained
    6 juniper berries
    3 eggs, a pinch of salt, a dash of tabasco

In a saucepan place the sausages, cover with drained sauerkraut and juniper berries which have been placed between layers of paper towel and cracked with a knife blade. Add 1 cup water and let braise for one hour. Let mixture cool and divide into four parts, each with one sausage and one-fourth of the sauerkraut. Cut each sausage into dime-size slices.

Make a basic omelet and jjust before rolling, carefully spread the sausage and sauerkraut mixture on the eggs. Roll onto a plate and serve with a glass of beer.

Portions of the sausage and sauerkraut mixture not used may be frozen for later use.

ORIENTAL OMELET
(serves 4)

    8 slices of bacon
    ½ cup chopped onion
    ½ cup cooked shrimp, diced fine
    ½ cup canned bean sprouts, washed and dried
    8 eggs
    4 tablespoons butter
    ¼ teaspoon tabasco

Sauce

Dissolve 2 tablespoons of cornstarch in 3 tablespoons of water. Add 2 teaspoons of soy sauce. Add this to 1 cup of strong bullion. Bring to a boil, stirring constantly. Set aside.

Cut the bacon strips across about 25 times. Place in a saucepan and fry until about 2 tablespoons of bacon fat has rendered itself from the bacon. Pour off this fat and continue to cook over medium heat. Add the chopped onion and cook until transparent— about 5 to 10 minutes. The bacon will appear a little brown. Add the shrimp and bean sprouts. Cook a few minutes and set aside.

Beat the eggs, add tabasco and a dash of salt.

Have your omelet pan on low heat. Turn to medium when you are ready to make the omelet. When hot, grease with 1 tablespoon butter, add 1 dipper or ½ cup of the beaten eggs to the buttered pan; add 1 heaping tablespoon of the bacon mixture to the batter in the pan and start the omelet with the scramble method. Roll onto a warm platter and place the omelets side by side. Heat the sauce and spoon over the omelets. Garnish with cress and serve immediately.

FLEMISH OMELET

    3 eggs
    1 tablespoon butter
    1 piece of Belgian endive
    1 shallot or 1 green onion (spring)

Melt the butter in a saucepan. Shred the endive and onion finely, or the chopped shallot, into the butter and cook until wilted. This takes a few minutes. Set aside.

If you use a teflon omelet pan this may be cooked in the omelet pan. Add to above mixture 1 teaspoon of chopped parsley. To this add the slightly beaten eggs with a dash of salt and tabasco. Scramble together in the usual way and roll onto a hot plate. Serve immediately.

OPERA HOUSE OMELET
For the Diet

    1 slice of eggplant, unpeeled, diced fine
    1 small onion the size of a nut, diced fine
    1 tablespoon of diced green pepper
    1 heaping tablespoon of diced tomato,
        peeled with seeds removed
    3 eggs, a dash of salt, ⅛ teaspoon tabasco

Place a 10″ CLUB ALUMINUM Teflon-coated omelet pan on low heat. Have a wooden salad fork on hand.

In a bowl beat the eggs till just blended and add the salt and tabasco. Adjust pan heat to medium. Rub a clove of garlic on the surface of the hot pan. Add to the pan 2 tablespoons of cooking oil.

First cook the eggplant, onions, and green pepper. Cook until the eggplant is soft when pressed with the wooden salad fork or rubber spatula.

Add the tomato and a scant ¼ teaspoon of sugar. Cook a few minutes, stirring constantly.

Pour the eggs into the mixture and quickly scramble the whole mixture with the salad fork, keeping the prongs of the fork flat on the bottom of the pan.

Some parmesan cheese may be sprinkled on this as an option. Roll omelet onto a warm plate and serve immediately.

ASPARAGUS OMELET

Cut the tender part of 2 stalks of cooked asparagus very fine. This will give you about 3 tablespoonfuls of finely cut asparagus.

Sauté this lightly in 1 tablespoon of butter, add 1 tablespoon of fines herbes.

Prepare 3 eggs for the basic omelet.

If you use a teflon pan, the asparagus may be sautéed in the omelet pan. Add the eggs and make the omelet. Just before rolling, sprinkle with parmesan cheese. Roll onto a hot dish.

Always use a wood fork or rubber wand on teflon pots and pans.

MUSHROOM OMELET

Chop 3 mushrooms. Saute in 1 tablespoon of oil, sprinkle with a little salt. The mushrooms will become moist. Sauté until the moisture has cooked away.

Make a basic omelet and to the eggs add the mushrooms.

Heat the pan and when ready add butter and dry or fresh tarragon—about 1 blade cut up or ¼ teaspoon if dry. Add the egg and mushroom mixture, scramble and roll out onto a hot plate.

RICE OMELET
(For one)

3 eggs
½ teaspoon salt (at least)
¼ teaspoon Tabasco
½ cup cooked rice
1 tablespoon chopped flat leaf parsley
2 tablespoons butter
½ cup grated cheese

Place the eggs in a bowl. Add the cooked rice, salt, and Tabasco. Have your omelet pan on medium so pan sides will be well heated.

Beat the eggs and other ingredients with a fork till just beaten through. Butter the pan. Add the egg mixture, *proceeding as with the basic recipe.* When the egg mixture appears set, spread evenly over the surface of the pan and sprinkle with Parmesan cheese (optional). Roll and eat while hot. Serve with Creole sauce or garnish with parsley.

CHICKEN LIVER OMELET
(For one or two)

½ pound fresh chicken livers
3 tablespoons butter
1 tablespoon chopped parsley
3 eggs
2 tablespoons dry sherry
¼ teaspoon salt
¼ teaspoon Tabasco

Trim the livers for foreign matter. Cut in half. In a sauté pan (small size) add 2 tablespoons of butter. Place on medium heat and let butter slowly get light brown. Add the livers and stir them quickly until brown all over, or about 5 minutes. Heat the sherry in a small flamer or small pot. Light and pour over the livers. Remove from fire and sprinkle with a little salt. These will be a garniture beside the omelet—not in it.

Take half of the pieces of liver (the total should be about 12 pieces) and chop the six pieces very fine. Set aside. Slice the remaining pieces and let set in the warm liquid. Beat the eggs in a bowl. Add salt, Tabasco, and chopped livers. Put a generous tablespoon of butter in your hot omelet pan. Add the parsley and sauté a minute. Add the egg mixture, and again with the circular motion stir the omelet till it thickens. Roll out onto a hot dish. Place the sliced livers and sauce next to omelet. Garnish with watercress.

VEAL KIDNEY OMELET
(For one or two)

3 eggs
1 veal kidney
3 tablespoons Madeira
½ cup stock
½ teaspoon salt
1 tablespoon parsley
4 tablespoons butter
⅛ teaspoon Tabasco
1 tablespoon chopped shallot
1 tablespoon cornstarch

Have the butcher skin the kidney and remove any foreign matter. *Split into 2 parts lengthwise, then slice very thin.* In a pan put 2 tablespoons of butter. On a medium heat make the butter quite brown but not black. Add the sliced kidney and mix till nicely brown, about 4 minutes. Remove from fire. Put kidney in a dish. In the pan make a sauce with 1 tablespoon of butter, 1 tablespoon of cornstarch. Mix over low flame. Add the chopped shallot and sauté for a minute. Remove pan from fire. Add ½ cup stock and the Madeira wine. Over a low heat, stir till it thickens, then add the kidneys. Season with ¼ teaspoon salt. Keep warm but set it aside.

Make the three-egg omelet seasoned with salt, Tabasco, and 1 tablespoon of chopped parsley. Turn onto a hot platter. Spoon the kidneys and their sauce around the omelet. Sprinkle with chopped parsley. Veal kidneys are really a garniture for the omelet and make a hearty main course dish.

CHEDDAR CHEESE OMELET
(For one or two)

3 eggs
1 tablespoon water
¼ teaspoon Tabasco (scant)
1 tablespoon butter
½ cup grated cheese
1 teaspoon chopped marjoram
¼ teaspoon salt

Place the eggs in a bowl. Add water, Tabasco, and salt. Have your pan on a medium heat. Omitting cheese, beat the eggs and other ingredients with a fork till just mixed. Butter the pan with a generous tablespoon of butter. It should bubble. Add the marjoram and sauté for a minute. Add the eggs. Proceed as with basic recipe till you spread the mixture over the pan. Make sure there are no holes.

Now sprinkle on the cheese. Then roll and serve.

OMELET WITH RED CAVIAR, SOUR CREAM
(For one)

>   3 eggs
> ¼ teaspoon salt (scant)
>   1 tablespoon chopped parsley
>   1 tablespoon red caviar
>   2 tablespoons sour cream
>   1 tablespoon water
>   1 tablespoon butter

Make the basic omelet and serve onto a hot plate. Then cut an incision lengthwise (about 3 inches long). Spread it a little and neatly spoon in your mixture of red caviar and sour cream. Sprinkle with parsley and eat hot.

SPINACH OMELET
(For one)

>   3 eggs
> ¼ teaspoon Tabasco (scant)
> ¼ teaspoon salt
>   2 tablespoons butter
>   3 tablespoons chopped, cooked (hot) spinach
>   3 tablespoons sour cream
>   1 teaspoon finely chopped onion
> ½ cup grated cheese

Have this spinach mixture ready to be stuffed into the omelet: In a saucepan place 1 tablespoon of butter, the finely chopped onion, and sauté over a low flame till just cooked—about 2 minutes. Do not brown. Add the chopped spinach and keep hot; add the sour cream and remove from burner.

Make the basic omelet in usual manner. Just before rolling, sprinkle with grated cheddar or your own favorite cheese. Roll to the edge of pan onto a hot dish. Make an incision and spread the omelet, spoon in the spinach mixture. This omelet, with some hot buttered Italian or French bread, and a glass of good white wine makes a most delightful luncheon.

[25]

MOUSSELINE OMELET
(A sweet for two)

    3 eggs
    1 tablespoon butter
    3 tablespoons sugar
    3 tablespoons apricot preserve

Separate the eggs. Beat the whites with 1 tablespoon of sugar till glossy and stiff. Using the same beater, beat the yolks with the remaining sugar till creamy and lemon colored. Combine both of these mixtures.

In hot omelet pan melt 1 tablespoon butter and pour in mixture. Spread over the entire surface of pan and when sides are brown, hold under the broiler to brown and set. Only takes one minute.

Spoon the apricot preserve close to the handle. With a spatula, fold over (rather than roll) onto a hot oval dish. Dust with confectioners' sugar and eat hot. May be flamed with 3 tablespoons of Irish Mist.

OMELET AUX CONFITURES

    3 eggs
    3 tablespoons sugar
    1 tablespoon butter
    3 tablespoons apricot preserves
    3 tablespoons Southern Comfort

Separate the eggs. Add *1 tablespoon of the sugar* to the egg yolks and beat with an electric or rotary beater until light, creamy and thick; with a clean, dry beater, beat the whites until they begin to show peaks, then gradually beat in the remaining sugar. Continue beating until the meringue is stiff and shiny. Fold the whites lightly into the yolk mixture with a rubber spatula.

Have omelet pan ready and add the butter. As it melts, grease right up to the edges of the pan so that the sides are buttered, too. Pour in the egg mixture and smooth the top with a spatula. Cook over a moderately high heat until the bottom is golden when the edge is lifted with a metal spatula. Place in a preheated broiler, not too close to the heat, until gilded on top. A matter of seconds. Don't even close the oven door.

Take out of the oven, spoon the apricot preserves onto the omelet close to the handle of the pan. Then, using a spatula, fold the omelet over once (do not attempt to roll up), then turn out on a heated platter. Sprinkle with sugar. Heat the Southern Comfort, ignite, and spoon over the omelet. Serve immediately. Serves 4.

QUEEN ANNE OMELET

⅔ cup canned applesauce
3 tablespoons kirsch
6 eggs
⅛ teaspoon cream of tartar
¼ cup sifted confectioners' sugar
1 cup granulated sugar
¼ cup toasted, slivered almonds

Combine the applesauce and *1 tablespoon of the kirsch*. Set aside. Have your omelet pan ready and buttered.

Separate *4 of the eggs*, place the whites in one bowl with the cream of tartar. Set aside for the moment. Combine the yolks in another large bowl *with the 2 whole eggs*. Beat with an electric beater or, preferably, in an electric mixer, adding the confectioners' sugar gradually. Continue beating until the mixture is as thick as mayonaise. Now beat the whites until fluffy, then add the granulated sugar very gradually. When all the sugar is in, continue to beat another 10 minutes until you have a thick, shiny meringue.

Fold the egg-yolk mixture into the meringue with a rubber spatula gently, but thoroughly. Divide the batter in half.

Make one omelet following basic instructions, page o. Slide the cooked omelet out of the pan onto a warm serving platter. *Do not roll up.* Spread with the applesauce. Set aside and keep warm. Make the second omelet and slide on top of the first. Cover with the meringue, sprinkle with the almonds and a little granulated sugar. Place in a preheated 450° F. oven for 5 minutes. Remove from the oven. Heat the remaining kirsch, ignite, and pour over the omelet. Serve immediately to 6.

STRAWBERRY OMELET

1 pint (2 cups) fresh ripe strawberries
4 tablespoons superfine sugar
1 tablespoon kirsch
2 eggs, separated

Wash, hull, dry and slice the strawberries. Mix in *2 tablespoons of the sugar* and allow them to stand until the strawberries become juicy. Then mix in the kirsch and set aside.

Combine the egg yolks with *1 tablespoon of the sugar* and beat with a rotary or electric beater until thick and creamy; beat the egg whites (use a clean, dry beater) until fluffy, then beat in the remaining sugar gradually and continue beating until the whites are stiff, smooth and shiny.

Fold the yolk mixture gently into the beaten whites. Have the omelet pan ready and heated with the butter *for one omelet*. Follow Basic Omelet instructions, page 0. When cooked, roll onto heated serving platter. Make a slit down the center, spoon half the strawberries into the slit, the remainder in a ribbon around the omelet. Serve at once. Serves 2.

LINGONBERRY OMELET FOR CHILDREN

2 eggs
1 tablespoon heavy cream
1 tablespoon sugar
2 dessert spoons lingonberry preserves or jelly
  Confectioners' sugar

Combine eggs, cream, and sugar in a bowl and beat with a rotary beater or whisk until light and fluffy. Have omelet pan ready, add butter *for one omelet,* and follow directions for cooking a Basic Omelet, page 0. After omelet has been turned out, make a slit down its length with a sharp knife and fill with the lingonberry preserves or jelly. Sift a little confectioners' sugar over the top and serve at once. Serves 1.

II

Crêpes

Crêpes are as versatile as omelets. They can turn leftovers into a most attractive main course; they can be rolled around all sorts of creamed fillings such as crab, lobster, chicken, or a julienne of vegetables, in a Velouté sauce to make an interesting first course; and dessert crêpes are, of course, real spectaculars.

To turn crêpes out with professional skill takes practice but the art is not difficult. The prime requisites are a good pan, a good recipe and enthusiasm.

> 4 eggs
> 1¼ cups sifted all-purpose flour
> 4 yolks
> 1 cup milk
> 1 tablespoon vegetable oil

Combine all ingredients in a large bowl and beat with a rotary beater until smooth. Tested between two fingers, the batter should feel as smooth as silk velvet and have the body and thickness of heavy cream. Cover and refrigerate for at least 1 hour, but better, 2. This quantity of batter makes about 24.

Note: If the batter is too thick, thin it down with milk, 1 tablespoon at a time, whisking constantly, until it reaches the right consistency.

The Important Steps in Making Crêpes

- Greasing the omelet pan. Crumple up a bit of wax paper, rub it over a stick of butter and grease the pan well. Always use butter.
- Place the pan over moderately high heat until it just reaches the smoking point. It is important to try and maintain this heat exactly. If the pan gets too hot, take off the heat long enough to allow it to cool down somewhat.

- Measure batter exactly so that all of the cooked crêpes are all of a size. A ladle is the most satisfactory of all implements if you can find one that holds 2 tablespoons (look in your silver drawer, there may be one there). Otherwise, use a measuring cup—a scant ¼ cup.

- The first crêpe is a sort of trial run to test the consistency of the batter, the pan, and the heat.

- Allow 2 tablespoons of batter of each crêpe. Pour it into the pan at the side away from you. Tilt the pan from side to side quickly so the batter covers the pan completely with a thin coating. Cook for 60 seconds or slightly longer.

- Lift up the edge of the crêpe with a spatula. If the underside is a light golden brown, pick up the crêpe with the tips of your fingers with both hands and flip it over (this is less hazardous than it may appear).

- Cook the second side for about 30 seconds. Actually, this second side will not brown like the first side but rather "freckle."

- Lift each crêpe as it's cooked from the pan with your fingers and stack on a plate, brown side up.

- Grease the pan lightly with butter between each crêpe.

- As you stack the crêpes, place a square of wax paper every sixth crêpe. This way you can keep track of the quantity without counting them individually. Useful if you are making a big batch.

CRÊPES STUFFED WITH LOBSTER IN PINK SAUCE

2 pounds lobster meat*
1 recipe for Béchamel Sauce [page 31]
3 tablespoons dry sherry
Salt
White pepper
24 crêpes [page 29]
Freshly grated Parmesan cheese

Cut the lobster meat in medium-size dice. Place in a saucepan with the 4 cups of Béchamel Sauce and the sherry. Season with salt and pepper to taste. Bring up to a boil but do not cook further. Strain the sauce from the lobsters through a colander into a large bowl (it'll be pink, you'll notice) leaving a light coating of sauce on the pieces. Return the strained sauce to the saucepan and keep warm.

Butter 2 pie plates or one 9 x 14-inch ovenproof baking dish. Place about 3 tablespoons of the lobster mixture in the center of each crêpe and fold all four sides over the filling, overlapping. Place the filled crêpes, fold-side down, in the baking dish as close together as possible. Cover with the pink sauce and place in a preheated 375° F. oven for ½ hour. Take out of the oven, sprinkle with the Parmesan, and place in a preheated broiler until the top is golden. Watch carefully so as not to brown it too much. It's just a matter of seconds. Serves 12.

* *Note:* If you are not going to cook the lobster meat yourself, lobsters are available in good fish markets freshly cooked in the shell, and as cooked lobster meat, fresh or frozen in 14-ounce pry-open, vacuum-sealed containers. In summer only, hand-picked, cooked, fresh lobster meat, chilled, is available (the whole lobster, lobster claws, tails or small, individual pieces).

BASIC MEDIUM-THICK BÉCHAMEL SAUCE

> 1 stick (8 tablespoons) butter
> ½ cup (tablespoons) all-purpose flour
> 4 cups milk, heated
> 1 teaspoon salt
> White pepper

Melt the butter over low heat, blend in the flour and cook slowly, stirring constantly, until the butter and flour froth together. About 2 minutes. Do not allow the *roux* to take on color. Take off the heat and add the milk all at once. Whisk briskly with a wire whip to incorporate the *roux* and liquid into a smooth mixture. Put back over high heat and cook, whipping steadily, until the sauce comes to a boil. Boil for 1 minute, whipping constantly. Add salt and pepper to taste. Makes 4 cups.

This is a medium-thick sauce that can be used as a base for many other sauces; with cream and dry sherry for fish; with tomato paste or puree for eggs, fish, chicken, vegetables; with curry for fish, veal, lamb, chicken, etc.

To make a thin Béchamel, allow 1 tablespoon of flour for each cup of liquid; for a soufflé Béchamel, allow 3 tablespoons of flour for each cup of liquid.

CRÊPES DE VOLAILLE

1 recipe crêpes [page 29]
1 5-pound poached chicken [page 33]
1 pound fresh mushroom buttons
2 tablespoons butter
4 cups Velouté Sauce [page 33]
½ teaspoon salt
¼ teaspoon white pepper
   Lemon juice
1 tablespoon fresh dill or fresh mixed herbs, finely chopped

Make the crêpes. This can be done ahead of time. Refrigerate or freeze, depending on when they are to be used.

Lift the cooled chicken from the broth. Strip the meat off the bones in large pieces, discarding bones, fat, and any gristle. Dice the chicken meat very fine. Place in a bowl and set aside momentarily.

Wipe the caps of the mushrooms with a clean, damp cloth; snip tips off the stems; quarter. Sauté [page 13]. Drain any mushroom juices from the pan over the chicken meat. Season the Velouté to taste with salt, pepper and a good squeeze of fresh lemon juice. Stir in the chopped dill or herbs. Pour over the chicken meat and combine well. Butter 2 pie plates or one 9 x 14-inch ovenproof baking dish. Place about 3 tablespoons of the chicken mixture in the middle of each crêpe (use the light side) and fold all four sides of the crêpe over the filling, overlapping. Place the filled crêpes, fold-side down, in the baking dish as close together as possible. Place in a preheated 375° F. oven for ¾ hour. Meanwhile, heat remaining Velouté. When the crêpes come out of the oven, cover with the hot Velouté and sprinkle lightly with finely-chopped mixed fresh herbs or dill. Serves 10.

The easy way to mince dill: Make little mounds of the lacy dill on a cutting board and cut across with a heavy, very sharp knife. Do not chop. Then mix together.

HOW TO POACH A CHICKEN

Combine 3 quarts cold water, 1 tablespoon salt, 1 slice of lemon, a few pieces of parsley, 1 onion, skin on, stuck with 2 cloves, a few pepercorns, 1 or 2 ribs of celery with tops, coarsely chopped, 1 carrot, scrubbed, coarsely chopped, a few gratings of fresh nutmeg in a big, heavy soup pot. Bring up to a boil, reduce heat to simmer, cover, and cook for 1 hour. Add a 5-pound chicken, at room temperature, and increase the heat. When broth comes to a boil again, reduce heat, cover, and simmer until the chicken is tender when pierced with a fork and the skin pulls away from the tips of the legs. About 1 hour. Take off heat, *remove cover,* and cool chicken in the stock quickly. In refrigerator or over a mixture of ice and water (like you do Champagne).

Note: A large 5- to 6-pound stewing chicken is less expensive than a young bird but takes about twice as long to cook. Many cooks believe you get a richer broth from these old birds.

VELOUTÉ SAUCE

This is one of the basic French sauces—essentially the same as a Béchamel (in America known as white sauce)—which is made with chicken, veal or fish stock (depending on how it is to be used) instead of milk.

    4 tablespoons (½ stick) butter
    ⅓ cup plus 1 tablespoon all-purpose flour
    4 cups chicken stock, heated, your own or
        canned condensed chicken broth
    ¼ teaspoon salt
      White pepper

Melt the butter in a heavy saucepan over low heat. When melted, stir in the flour until smooth and cook slowly, stirring, until the butter and flour froth together without taking on color. About 2 minutes. Take off the heat, and whip in the hot broth to blend the *roux* and the stock together. Place over a moderately high heat and bring up to a boil, stirring with the whisk. Then boil for 1 minute, still stirring. Take off the heat and beat in salt and pepper to taste.

Note: If the Velouté must stand briefly, place Saran wrap flat on top of the sauce to prevent a skin forming or butter top, as French chefs do, by rubbing top lightly with a stick of firm butter. Do not cover.

To keep hot or reheat, place over simmering water; to keep briefly, refrigerate; to store, freeze.

CRÊPES STUFFED WITH CHEESE

Mix together ½ cup Béchamel sauce, ½ cup softened roquefort cheese, ⅛ teaspoon nutmeg and a pinch of black pepper.

Place 1 heaping tablespoon of the mixture onto each crêpe and spread over the entire crêpe with a spatula.

Roll and place the crêpes side by side in a buttered oven-proof dish. Sprinkle the filled crêpes with grated Gruyere or Parmesan cheese.

Place under broiler as far as possible from the flame until cheese is melted and golden brown.

DESSERT CRÊPE BATTER

Sift into a mixing bowl 1 cup flour with 2 tablespoons fine sugar.

Add 4 whole eggs, one at a time, and whisk or use a rotary beater until the mixture is smooth. Gradually add 1 cup of milk and ¼ cup of water. Whisk in 1 tablespoon of Mazola or Wesson oil and continue to whisk until smooth. Set aside for 30 minutes.

The consistency should be like heavy cream.

If this crêpe batter is to be used for dessert, beat in 1 tablespoon of liqueur—Cointreau or Curaçao.

I recommend this batter for all types of fruit-filled crêpes.

SUZETTE SAUCE

Onto wax paper grate finely zest of:

> 1 lemon
> 1 orange
> 1 lime

Squeeze the juice into a small bowl and set aside.

Melt one stick of butter in a Teflon or aluminum pan over low heat. Add 1 cup of superfine sugar, and the fruit juice; bring to a boil and simmer for two minutes. Stir in three tablespoons of dark rum or brandy.

Lay out eight crêpes and in the centre of each place a heaping tablespoon of cut fint fruit: fresh peaches, bananas, etc. Roll and place in the pan side by side.

Spoon sauce over each crêpe over low flame.

In a small saucepan heat 4 tablespoons of Irish Mist. Pour over the crêpes, set alight, spoon sauce over each crêpe and serve flaming.

CRÊPES FILLED WITH CURRANT JELLY

Cream ½ cup sweet butter (1 stick) with 2 tablespoons Kirsch and 2 teaspoons lemon juice. Stir in ½ cup red currant jelly.

Have ready 8 crêpes. Lay the crêpes on a board—pale side up and spread with a heaping tablespoon of the mixture, fold or roll and place side by side in an oblong oven-proof dish.

Sprinkle with granulated sugar, and place under a broiler until the sugar is caramelized.

Serve immediately.

CRÊPES STUFFED WITH PRUNES

Cook 1 pound of prunes with 2 slices of lemon and 1 clove until very soft. Drain, remove pits and press through a coarse sieve or purée in a blender. You should have 2 cups of purée.

Sweeten to taste with about ¼ cup fine sugar and 1 teaspoon of grated zest of lemon, using a firm lemon and the fine part of your grater. The white part of the lemon is inclined to give off a bitter taste.

Pass ¼ cup of blanched almonds through the moulle and add to the prune mixture. Pour into a buttered baking dish or Corning oven-proof platter and place in a pre-heated oven (250°) for 20 minutes. Remove from oven and flame with a prune liqueur.

Yield: 12 crêpes.

CRÊPES FILLED WITH FRANGIPANE CREAM

In a saucepan mix ½ cup flour and ¾ cup sugar. Stir in 2 whole eggs, plus 2 yolks. Mix to a smooth paste.

Scald 2 cups milk and gradually stir into the paste. Cook the mixture, stirring constantly till it comes to a boil, for 2 minutes, or until it begins to bubble over low heat. Remove from flame and set in a pan of crushed ice. Stir in 2 tablespoons of oleo or butter, and add ½ teaspoon vanilla and 4 hard macaroons finely crushed.

Cool and fill each crêpe. Yield: 12 crêpes.

CRÊPES WITH CHOCOLATE CREAM

In a mixing bowl beat with a rotary beater 3 eggs and 1 cup of sugar until light and creamy.

Melt in a saucepan ½ pound sweet butter over low flame and add 4 ounces of Bakers chocolate (semi-sweet), but do not allow to bubble.

Add to the egg and sugar mixture and when blended place in a bowl of crushed ice, beating until creamy and thick.

Fill each crêpe with a heaping tablespoon of the filling, roll and place side by side in a buttered oblong baking dish.

Heat 1 cup of orange marmalade until thin, pour over the crêpes, sprinkle with finely chopped walnuts or almonds.

Place in a preheated oven (250°) for 10 minutes.

Remove, and just before serving, flame with 3 tablespoons of heated Grand Marnier.

CRÊPES WITH SEEDLESS GRAPES

2 cups green seedless grapes, cut in half
1 cup sour cream
2 tablespoons sugar

Mix the above ingredients. Fill six or eight crêpes—pale side up. Roll the crêpes and place in a buttered oblong baking dish.

Brush with melted sweet butter and place in a pre-heated oven (350°) for 20 minutes.

Remove from oven, sprinkle with granulated sugar and place under broiler for a few minutes, or until sugar is caramelized. Serve immediately.

[36]

III

Menu One

FOR 12 GUESTS

Shrimp Toast   Beef Fingers

Individual Tomato Cheese Soufflés

Chicken Kiev

Stuffed Mushroom Caps   Quattrochenni

Bavarian Cream with Apricot Rosettes

---

*The menus in these chapters are designed to set your own imagina-
tion going because availability of produce varies with geography. I've
given only the dinner recipes I feel might be hard to find and most of
my dishes are the ones I have prepared for my clients in New York,
Dallas, Chicago, and New Orleans. All of them are yours to try, to
experiment with, and to enjoy. Bon Appetite!*

SHRIMP TOAST

    1 pound raw shrimp
    1 can (8-ounce size) water chestnuts, minced
    2 scallions, minced
    1 teaspoon minced fresh ginger root
    1 teaspoon salt
    ½ teaspoon sugar
    1 tablespoon cornstarch
    1 egg, slightly beaten
    1 tablespoon sherry
    6 slices 2-day old bread
    2 cups vegetable oil

Shell, devein, wash and drain shrimp. Mince very fine. Combine thoroughly with water chestnuts, scallions, ginger root, salt, sugar, cornstarch, egg and sherry.

Cut the crusts off the bread, then cut into four triangles. Spread 1 heaping teaspoon on the shrimp mixture on each triangle. Heat oil to 375° F. on thermometer. Gently lower the triangles, shrimp side down, into the hot fat and cook half a minute; turn and fry a few more seconds. Shrimp Toast should be golden brown when perfectly cooked. Drain on paper towels. Serve immediately, or keep warm in a low oven.

BEEF FINGERS

    4 slices toast
    ¼ teaspoon Tabasco
    ⅛ cup water
    1 teaspoon salt
    1 pound top round steak, ground, no fat
    3 tablespoons of chili sauce or catsup

Toast the bread in a toaster (not the oven) until medium brown but not completely dried out. Combine Tabasco, water and salt, then mix into the ground meat well with wet hands. Form into four balls, place on toast and flatten with the palm of your hand to the same shape as the piece of toast.

With a wet knife, cut through the center of each slice; then turn and cut across in three even slices to make six fingers. Make an indentation in the meat in the center of each "finger" with a demi-tasse spoon or your finger. Fill with either chili sauce or catsup.

Using a spatula, place the Beef Fingers on a cookie sheet and place under a preheated broiler for 4 to 5 minutes. Serve piping hot.

INDIVIDUAL TOMATO CHEESE SOUFFLÉS

- 14 large firm tomatoes, all of a size
- 4 tablespoons (½ stick) butter
- 3 tablespoons flour
- 1 cup milk
- ½ teaspoon salt
- ¼ teaspoon Tabasco
- 1 cup grated Cheddar cheese
- 4 eggs, separated

Prepare the tomatoes like this: Wash, dry, turn stemside down and cut a slice off the bottom—approximately 3 inches in diameter. Then, with a spoon scoop out the pulp leaving a shell about ½-inch thick. Sprinkle with salt, invert and allow the tomatoes to drain.

Melt the butter in a heavy saucepan, then stir in the flour and cook until the butter foams. Take off the fire, mix in the milk and cook over a moderate heat, stirring constantly with a wooden spoon, until the sauce is very thick. Take off the heat, stir in the salt, Tabasco and cheese. Set aside.

While sauce is cooling, turn the tomatoes right side up and wrap an aluminum foil collar (5 x 12 inches) around each tomato, pinching it together to make it hold. The collar should stand about 2 inches above the cavity.

Now add the egg yolks, one at a time, to the cooled sauce, beating very hard after each addition. Add a pinch of salt to the egg whites and beat with an electric or rotary beater until the whites stand in peaks when you hold up the beater. Add about a third of the beaten egg whites to the cheese sauce and whisk them in vigorously with a wire whisk. Fold in remaining egg whites gently. Spoon mixture into the tomatoes, filling them to the top; place on baking sheets and bake in a preheated 350° F. oven for 40 minutes.

To serve, remove the foil, arrange soufflés on a warm serving platter and garnish with bouquets of watercress.

CHICKEN KIEV

12 whole breasts of chicken, with or without the main wing bones attached
¾ pound (3 sticks) butter, well chilled
   Salt
   Pepper
4 tablespoons parsley and chives, finely chopped
7 eggs, slightly beaten
1 cup flour
3 cups fresh bread crumbs
   Fat for deep frying (about 3 pounds)
   Watercress

Have the butcher bone and halve the chicken breasts. Place the breasts between pieces of wax paper and pound with a mallet until thin, taking care not to break the flesh. Remove from paper.

Cut the cold butter into 12 finger-shaped pieces (each finger will be ¼ of a stick or 2 tablespoons). Just at the wing bone, place a finger of butter in each breast, sprinkle with salt and pepper and ½ teaspoon of the fresh herbs. Roll chicken up very tightly, allowing the wing bone to protrude. Dredge each roll lightly with flour, dip into beaten eggs, and roll in bread crumbs. Refrigerate for at least 1 hour before frying. This helps to make the bread crumbs adhere.

Heat the shortening in a deep fryer or kettle to 360° F. on thermometer. Cook 3 to 4 pieces at a time if the fryer will accommodate that many. Don't crowd the fryer or you won't get proper browning. Brown on all sides, which should take 4 to 5 minutes. Drain on paper towelling. Arrange in deep chop platter, heated, with a garnish of watercress.

STUFFED MUSHROOM CAPS

    24 large mushrooms with stems
     3 tablespoons salad oil
     1 small onion, chopped very fine
    ¼ pound salami, tongue or ham, diced
    ½ teaspoon salt
       Freshly-ground pepper
    ½ cup fresh bread crumbs
     1 egg, slightly beaten
    ½ cup freshly-grated Parmesan cheese
       Butter, softened

Wash mushrooms under tepid running water, then dry thoroughly. Break off stems and chop very fine. Set caps aside.

Heat oil in skillet, add the chopped mushrooms and onion and sauté for about 5 minutes. Take off the fire and mix with the diced meat, salt and pepper to taste, and bread crumbs. Then mix in eggs and cheese thoroughly. Butter the inside of the mushrooms and fill with the mixture, allowing about 1 tablespoon for each cap.

Place on a cookie sheet and bake in a 375° F. oven for 20 minutes.

QUATTROCHENNI

     6 packages frozen chopped spinach
     1 cup egg pastina
    ½ pound bacon
    ½ cup Parmesan cheese
       Salt
       Pepper
       Nutmeg
    ¼ pound (1 stick) butter

Cook the spinach according to package directions, then drain thoroughly. Bring 1 quart salted water to a boil, add the pastina and when water comes to a boil again, boil exactly 5 minutes. Take off the heat, add cold water to stop the cooking, and drain very well.

Cut the bacon slices into thirds, place in a large frying pan and fry until nicely brown and crisp. Drain off the fat, add the cooked spinach, pastina, cheese, salt, pepper and nutmeg to taste, and butter. Mix very well and spoon into a heated vegetable dish.

BAVARIAN CREAM

3 packages unflavored gelatin
6 cups cold milk
6 eggs, separated
¾ cup sugar
2 tablespoons vanilla or brandy
2 cans (1-pound size) apricot halves, drained
2 cups heavy cream
6 tablespoons Cointreau
6 tablespoons sugar

Dissolve gelatin in *1 cup cold milk*. Set aside. Pour remaining milk into a heavy saucepan and bring to a boil slowly. Meanwhile, beat egg yolks until very thick in a large bowl, adding the sugar at little at a time. Take hot milk off the stove, stir in about a cupful to the yolk mixture, then add the remaining milk, stirring constantly. Put back over the heat and cook slowly, stirring constantly with a wooden spatula until it is about as thick as heavy cream. Take off the heat and stir in the softened gelatin. Set aside to cool, then add the vanilla or brandy. Place in refrigerator until almost firm.

Add a pinch of salt to the egg whites and beat with electric or rotary beater until whites stand in peaks when you lift up the beater. Then fold gently into the gelatin mixture.

Rinse out two ring molds with cold water, drain, and spoon in the Bavarian Cream. Refrigerate until firm.

To serve: Turn Bavarian Cream out onto handsome serving platters, fill centers with drained apricots and garnish around the rings with apricot rosettes.

To make rosettes: Beat cream until stiff, beat in the sugar, then stir in the Cointreau. Pipe the cream into the apricot halves.

IV

Menu Two

FOR 12 GUESTS

Bacon Sticks   Onion Pinwheel Sandwiches

Sole Joinville

Roast Duck with Black Cherries

Stuffed Artichoke Hearts   Braised Cucumbers, Tarragon

Apple Charlotte with Vanilla Sauce

BACON STICKS

1 pound thinly-sliced bacon
1 box Pan'dor bread sticks

Bring bacon to room temperature. Then carefully wrap the bacon around each bread stick from one end to the other. When bacon is warm, you will find it will stretch.

Place the sticks on a broiling rack on a cookie sheet and bake in a preheated 350° F. oven until bacon is golden brown and crisp. Arrange on a napkin lined serving dish, log fashion, and serve at once.

ONION PINWHEEL SANDWICHES

Unsliced, firm-textured bread
Mayonnaise
Italian onions
Salt and pepper
Minced parsley

The quantities you need depend on the number of people you will serve, but it is well to know these incredibly good sandwiches disappear like the proverbial snow. So, make up far more than seems like good sense. Two people can accomplish this job more easily and more efficiently than one, since it can be worked more or less on the assembly line method.

Slice bread very thin, spread both sides with mayonnaise, place thinly-sliced onions between the two halves, sprinkle with salt and pepper, then cut with 1½-inch cookie cutter.

Have on the side a bowl of mayonnaise and a bowl of minced parsley. Roll the edges of the sandwiches in the mayonnaise, then roll in the minced parsley. Arrange on serving plate, pyramid fashion (a cake stand is very effective).

Wrap in a fresh cloth wrung out in cold water and refrigerate until ready to serve.

SOLE JOINVILLE

12 pieces fillet of sole
3 pounds fresh salmon, boned and skinned
1 cup heavy cream
⅛ teaspoon mace
1 teaspoon salt
24 uncooked shrimp, shelled and deveined
2 cups dry white wine and 2 cups of water
1 onion, chopped
    Few sprigs parsley
¼ teaspoon Tabasco
24 mushrooms
½ cup salad oil
½ cup (1 stick) butter
½ cup flour
1 tablespoon paprika or tomato paste

Butter two 8-inch ring mold pans. Line molds with strips of sole, skin side up, overlapping slightly so there is no gap between.

Put the salmon through the meat grinder, using the finest blade, then combine with cream, mace and salt, mixing thoroughly. Spoon into the lined ring molds, folding ends of sole over the mixture. Cover with wax paper or foil and tie securely. Place in a pan of hot water (the water should reach to about half the depth of the mold) and bake in a 350° F. oven for 30 minutes.

Meanwhile, wash shrimp and place in a saucepan with 2 cups of water, the wine, onion, parsley and Tabasco. Bring to a boil. Take off the heat and drain, reserving the broth. Keep warm.

Wash mushrooms. If large, quarter; if small, leave whole. Heat oil in a frying pan and sauté the mushrooms for about 5 minutes. Drain. Set aside and keep warm. Melt the butter, stir in the flour and cook until butter foams. Take off the heat and stir in the fish broth until smooth. Return to heat and bring to a boil. Sauce should be about as thick as heavy cream. If too thick, correct by the addition of a little cream. Then stir in the paprika or tomato paste to "pink" the sauce.

When molds are cooked, turn out onto serving platters. Fill centers with shrimp and mushrooms. Spoon the sauce over the whole dish with a little extra over the shrimp and mushrooms. Garnish with watercress.

ROAST DUCK WITH BLACK CHERRIES

4 ducks, quartered
5 tablespoons salad oil
1 carrot, sliced
1 stalk celery, sliced
1 onion, sliced
3 tablespoons flour
2 cups of broth
    or 2 cups water and 2 tablespoons meat glaze
2 tablespoons tomato paste
2 cans (1 pound, 14-ounce size) black pitted cherries
1 cup port wine
½ cup currant jelly
1 tablespoon cornstarch

Place pieces of duck in roasting pans, bone side down. Bake in a preheated 375° F. oven for 1½ hours. At this point, drain off all the fat and place under a preheated broiler until skin gets crisp and brown. Keep warm in a low oven.

In a saucepan combine oil, carrot, celery, and onion and braise until slightly browned. Stir in the flour until smooth and cook 2 or 3 minutes. Take off the heat, add the broth (or water and meat glaze) and tomato paste. Return to range and cook over a moderate heat for 30 minutes. Set demi-glaze aside.

Meanwhile, drain the cherries and boil the juice down to half. Mix the cornstarch with a little water, stir into the reduced cherry juice and cook over a medium heat until sauce has thickened. Stir in the port wine and currant jelly. Strain the demi-glaze into the cherry sauce, add the cherries, bring to a boil, then simmer for 5 minutes.

Place duck pieces on a warm serving platter, spoon the hot cherry sauce over all and arrange the Stuffed Artichokes around the edge.

STUFFED ARTICHOKE HEARTS

    4 packages frozen peas, thawed
    1 teaspoon salt
  ½ teaspoon white pepper
    2 cans (14-ounce size) artichoke hearts
  ½ cup (1 stick) butter
    4 tablespoons flour

Purée peas in electric blender. Add salt and pepper. Place in top of double boiler and keep hot.

Open artichoke cans, drain and dry thoroughly with paper towels.

Place butter in a large heavy skillet and heat until it foams. Do not brown. Sauté the artichoke hearts, not too many at a time, quickly. Place on a baking sheet as they finish cooking.

Stir flour into butter remaining in the pan until smooth. Take off the heat and mix in the puréed peas, mixing very thoroughly. Using a tube, pipe the pea into the artichoke hearts. Keep warm until ready to arrange on platter with ducks.

BRAISED CUCUMBERS, TARRAGON

  12 cucumbers or zucchini
  ½ cup (1 stick) butter
    1 tablespoon dry tarragon
    1 teaspoon salt
       Freshly-ground black pepper

Peel the cucumbers, cut lengthwise in quarters and remove the seeds with a spoon. Now cut the quarters into ½-inch pieces.

Melt butter in a large skillet and bring to a foam, but do not brown. Add the cucumbers, sprinkle with salt and stir in the tarragon. Cook over a high heat, stirring with a wooden spoon, for 5 minutes or until you hear it "sing." Spoon into a warm vegetable dish and season with a few twists of the pepper mill.

12 cooking apples
1 tablespoon lemon juice
1 teaspoon cinnamon
1½ cups sugar
½ cup apricot or pineapple jam
2 loaves firm-textured bread (about 30 slices)
1 cup (2 sticks) sweet butter, softened

Vanilla Sauce

1 cup heavy cream
2 tablespoons brandy
1 pint vanilla ice cream, softened

Peel and core apples and cut into small pieces. Add lemon juice, cinnamon, sugar and apricot or pineapple jam. Combine well and set aside. Trim crusts off bread and cut all, except two, in half. Take the two whole slices and cut into circles, using a saucer as a guide. These go in the bottom of the molds. Spread all the bread with softened butter. Butter two charlotte molds or any 6-cup metal molds.

Melt 2 tablespoons butter in a large skillet and brown the bread, buttered side down, lightly, over a medium heat. Take 5 of these slices and cut into croutons. Return them to the pan and brown well. Stir into the apple mixture.

To line the molds, first place the circles of bread in the bottom, then arrange the pieces around the sides, allowing them to overlap slightly at the bottom. No part of the molds should show. Fill the molds with the apple mixture, cover the top with the remaining pieces of bread. Cover with foil and secure.

Place on the middle rack of a preheated 375° F. oven and bake for 1 hour. Remove foil, turn off the oven, and leave the Charlottes in the oven another 10 minutes.

To serve, turn molds out on, preferably, round platters.

To make Vanilla Sauce: Beat cream. When thick and heavy, stir in brandy. Then combine with ice cream that has just begun to get soft. Spoon into serving bowl and serve with the hot Apple Charlotte.

V

Menu Three

Cheese Grill

Fillet of Beef in Aspic with Truffles

Sweet and Sour Red Snapper

Fried Rice, Chinese Style

Moussaka

Spinach Salad

Baked Alaska   Strawberries Melba

CHEESE GRILL

2½ cups coarsely grated Parmesan cheese
½ cup commercial mayonnaise
1 small onion, minced very fine
3 to 4 drops Tabasco
5 slices toast

Mix cheese, onion, Tabasco and mayonnaise together into a thick paste. Spread on the toast. Then, with a wet knife, cut into triangles. With a spatula, lift onto a cookie sheet and place in a preheated broiler, not too close to the flame, until lightly browned. Serve at once.

FILLET OF BEEF IN ASPIC WITH TRUFFLES

6 to 7 pounds short end of fillets of beef
   Salt
3 cans beef consommé
2 envelopes unflavored gelatin
1 small can of truffles, drained and cut in julienne
   Watercress

Place beef in a preheated 425° F. oven and roast for 10 minutes, meat side down. Turn, sprinkle with salt and continue roasting another 30 minutes (a total of 40 minutes altogether). Take out of the oven and cool.

Sprinkle the gelatin over ½ cup cold water to soften. Bring the consommé to a boil, take off the heat, and stir in the gelatin until completely dissolved. Pour all but 1 cup of the consommé into a shallow pan and refrigerate until it is firm. When firm, cut in small diamond shapes. Chill the remaining cup over ice until of the consistency of white of egg.

Slice the beef and arrange on a platter, spoon the chilled consommé over the beef slices, sprinkle with the julienned truffles, surround with the aspic diamonds and garnish with a handsome bouquet of watercress.

SWEET AND SOUR RED SNAPPER

Sauce

- 2 tablespoons salad oil
- 2 cloves garlic, split
- 3 tablespoons vinegar
- 3 tablespoons soy sauce
- 4 tablespoons ketchup
- 6 tablespoons sugar
- 2 cups chicken broth
- 3 tablespoons cornstarch
- ½ cup cooked peas
- ½ cup cooked carrots
- 1 small can water chestnuts, drained and diced
- 1 small can shrimp, drained

To prepare fish

- 4 red snappers or 4 sea bass, about 2½ pounds each
- ½ cup flour
- 1 teaspoon salt
- Oil for deep frying

To make sauce: Heat oil in saucepan, add garlic; when brown, remove and discard.

Mix together vinegar, soy sauce, ketchup, sugar and chicken broth. Add to oil in pan. Bring to a boil. Add cornstarch mixed with a little water and cook, over moderate heat, stirring constantly, until sauce has thickened. Add carrots, peas, water chestnuts and shrimp. Set aside and keep warm.

Have the fish monger fillet the fish, leaving the skin intact. Score the flesh or inside of each fillet just as you would ham. Salt the fillets, then coat with flour, shaking off any excess.

Heat oil in fryer to 375° F. on thermometer and fry the fillets a few at a time (don't crowd the pan) about 5 to 6 minutes. Drain on paper towels and keep warm.

When all the fish is cooked, arrange on a large warm platter and spoon the sauce over all. Serve with Fried Rice, Chinese Style.

2 eggs, slightly beaten
4 tablespoons salad oil
½ cup chopped scallions, green tops only
6 cups cold cooked rice
1½ tablespoons soy sauce
½ teaspoon sugar
¼ teaspoon Ac'cent
½ cup diced roast pork or ham

Scramble the eggs slightly in *1 tablespoon* of oil. Set aside to use later on.

In a heavy frying pan over a high flame, heat the remaining oil, add scallions and stir a few times. Next add rice (it is important for the rice to be completely cold before adding to skillet, otherwise the grains will stick together) and stir quickly so rice does not stick to the pan and will be well coated with the oil. Add soy sauce, sugar, and Ac'cent. Mix well. Finally, add the meat and the eggs, mixing and breaking the eggs into little pieces into the rice. Serve immediately or keep warm in a very low oven.

This is the basic Chinese method of cooking fried rice. Any cooked meat, diced, can be used instead of roast pork; ham, chicken, roast beef, roast veal or boiled shrimp.

MOUSSAKA

3 pounds chuck steak, coarsely ground
1 small onion, chopped
½ whole nutmeg, grated
2 tomatoes, peeled, seeded and coarsely chopped
8 baby zucchini and 4 small eggplants
½ cup salad oil
Salt
Few drops Tabasco
1 pound Parmesan cheese, grated
½ cup (1 stick) butter
½ cup flour
1 quart milk

Place meat in a large, heavy kettle, add about 3 tablespoons water, and cook over moderate heat until crumbly—about 10 minutes. Add the chopped onion, nutmeg, and chopped tomatoes and cook 20 minutes. Set aside.

Trim ends off zucchini and eggplants, then slice in thin pieces. Heat the salad oil in a large skillet until it literally starts to smoke. Add the zucchini and eggplant and cook, over high heat, stirring constantly until vegetables are almost a mush. Season with a little salt and Tabasco. Spread in a large flat baking dish approximately 9 x 14 inches. Sprinkle with a little of the grated Parmesan. Set aside for a moment.

Melt the butter in a saucepan, stir in the flour until well blended and cook until butter foams. Take off the heat, add the milk, return to heat and bring to a boil slowly, stirring constantly. Cook for about 5 minutes, still stirring, or until the sauce has thickened. Season with about 1 teaspoon salt.

Spread the meat mixture over the vegetable, sprinkle with more of the cheese. Spoon the white sauce over all and cover with the remaining cheese. Place in a preheated 375° F. oven and bake for 1 hour or until golden brown.

Serve immediately or keep warm in a very low oven.

SPINACH SALAD

Dressing

   1 cup olive oil
   ⅓ cup tarragon vinegar
   1 whole egg
   1 tablespoon meat glaze
   1 small white onion, chopped
   1 teaspoon salt
     Few drops Tabasco

Salad

   2 pounds fresh spinach or 1 pound each romaine
       and spinach
   1 cup French dressing
   1 cup (11-ounce size) Mandarin oranges, drained
   ½ pound bacon, fried

To make dressing: Place all ingredients in the container of the electric blender, turn to high, and blend for 1 minute. Store in jar.

Wash spinach and cut off heavy ribs. Dry very well between fresh towels.

Cut bacon into small pieces with scissors, then fry until crisp and brown. Drain well.

Place spinach or spinach and romaine in a large salad bowl, scatter the Mandarin oranges and bacon crisps on top. Just before serving, add 1 cup of the dressing. Toss very well.

BAKED ALASKA

2 packages layer sponge cake
1 quart vanilla ice cream, softened
1 quart chocolate ice cream, softened
8 egg whites
  Pinch salt
2 cups sugar
2 cans (5-ounce size) toasted, slivered almonds

Place a layer of the sponge cake on a cookie sheet, spread a good inch layer of vanilla ice crea mon top, cover with a second layer of cake, add a layer of chocolate ice cream, also an inch thick. Place in freezing compartment of your refrigerator while you prepare the second cake in exactly the same way. When second cake is complete, put it, too, in the freezing compartment.

Add a pinch of salt to the egg whites and beat until the whites stand in peaks when you hold up the beater. Add the sugar very gradually, beating steadily with electric or rotary beater until mixture is very glossy and holds firm points.

Take cakes from refrigerator, one at a time, and cover completely with the meringue, reserving a small amount for decorating, using a rose tube. When cakes are frosted, sprinkle with the slivered almonds, place in a preheated 500° F. oven until the meringue is flecked with gold. About 3 to 5 minutes. Return to freezer until you are ready to serve, or serve immediately.

STRAWBERRIES MELBA

  6 pints large strawberries
  4 packages frozen raspberries, thawed and drained
  ½ cup sugar
  ⅓ cup kirsch

Wash strawberries under tepid running water, then lift out of the water with your hands and drain on paper towels. When dry, hull.

Place the drained raspberries in the container of the electric blender. Turn to low and blend for 1 minute, add the sugar and blend another 2 minutes, add the kirsch and blend 1 more minute. Strain through a very fine sieve to eliminate all the seeds.

Arrange strawberries in a crystal or silver compote in a pyramid, spoon the raspberry sauce over all. Serve with whipped cream.

VI

Menu Four

Endive in Ham Rolls with Cheese Sauce

Roast Rack of Lamb   Fruit Mint Garnish

Hominy Grit Soufflé   Chinese Broccoli

Chocolate Roll with Chocolate Sauce

Almond Roll

Coffee

ENDIVES IN HAM ROLLS WITH CHEESE SAUCE

14 heads Belgian endive
1 cup chicken stock, your own or canned condensed
    chicken broth
Juice 1 lemon
Salt
14 thin slices baked ham

Trim the bottoms of the endives and discard any withered leaves. Wash, one by one, under cold running water. Drain thoroughly. Place in a large, heavy skillet with the chicken stock, lemon juice and salt. Bring to a boil, cover with a round of buttered wax paper, then the lid of the pan. Reduce heat to simmer and cook until the endives are tender. About 30 minutes. Take off the heat and drain very thoroughly. When cool enough to handle, roll each endive up in a slice of ham, and place, *fold side down*, on a baking sheet. Set aside.

Now, make the *Cheese Sauce:*

1 stick (8 tablespoons) butter
½ cup all-purpose flour, scant
4 cups milk, heated
1 teaspoon salt
½ teaspoon white pepper
1 cup freshly grated Swiss cheese

Melt the butter in a large, heavy saucepan. Stir in the flour until smooth. Add the milk, salt and pepper. Put back over the heat, bring up to a boil, reduce heat and simmer for 3 minutes, stirring constantly with a whisk or spatula or until the sauce bubbles and thickens slightly. Take off the heat, cool, and stir in ¾ *cup of the grated cheese.*

Cover the bottom of an ovenproof baking dish, that can go to the table, with a layer of the Cheese Sauce. The dish should be just large enough to accommodate the ham rolls flat, but close together. Place the rolls on top of the sauce and spoon the remaining sauce over all. Sprinkle with the remaining cheese. Place in a preheated broiler away from the flame until the sauce is lightly gilded. The dish can remain in a very low oven, about 200° F., until serving time. Serves 12 to 14.

Note: By itself, this makes a very good luncheon dish.

ROAST RACK OF LAMB

In ordering a rack of lamb (there are 16 chops), have the butcher remove the chine bone and any gristle, leaving a small covering of fat on the back. At the same time, have him scrape the ends of the chops as you do for French chops, then crack each chop between the ribs. Be sure to ask for paper frills to place on the rib tips before serving.

Heat a large, heavy skillet until very hot, then brown the fat side of the rack until rich and golden. This can be done ahead of time and the meat set aside until roasting time.

Rub the roast with a mixture of salt, freshly-ground pepper and dried tarragon. Then wrap the rib tips with foil to keep them from burning. Place the prepared roast, fat side up, in a large roasting pan, in a preheated 400° F. oven. Roast 40 minutes or until the lamb is pink (140° F. on a meat thermometer); 50 minutes for well done (160° F. on a meat thermometer).

Take out of the oven and place on a large, hot serving platter and allow the meat to rest about 10 minutes so the juices can settle. Remove the foil from tips and replace with the paper frills. Arrange the Fruit Mint Garnish around the rack, with sprigs of fresh watercress, just before taking it to the table.

Note: Always serve lamb on very hot plates because it tends to cool more quickly than other meats.

ORANGE MINT GARNISH

Slice off the ends of 3 navel oranges, then slice each orange into 4 even slices. Place on a cookie sheet.

Peel and core 3 Rome Beauty apples, then slice each one into 4 even slices. Melt 2 tablespoons of butter in a skillet and sauté the apple slices lightly—do not overcook. Lift with a spatula onto the orange slices, then place 1 teaspoon of mint jelly in the center of each apple. Makes 12.

HOMINY GRITS SOUFFLÉ

      Butter
      Freshly grated Parmesan cheese
  ¾ cup hominy grits
  2 cups milk
  ¼ stick (4 tablespoons) butter
  6 eggs, separated

Butter a 1-quart soufflé dish thoroughly, including all the "corners" and coat with the grated Parmesan, dumping out any excess. Chill in the refrigerator or, if you're short of time, in the freezer.

Pour the grits into *1 cup of boiling water in the top* of the double boiler and cook for 2 minutes. Stir in *1 cup of the milk*, place over boiling water and cook for 30 minutes. Then stir in the remaining milk and the butter until well combined and piping hot. Take off the heat. Cool.

Beat the egg yolks into the lukewarm grits mixture, one at a time, vigorously.

Beat the egg whites until they are stiff and shiny when you hold the beater straight up. Whisk about a third into the grits mixture, then fold in the remainder carefully with a rubber spatula. Pour into the prepared soufflé dish and place in a preheated 350° F. oven for 45 minutes. Serve immediately.

Serves 12 as an accompaniment to the meat course.

GRACE CHU'S BROCCOLI, CHINESE STYLE

  2 bunches broccoli
  4 tablespoons peanut or vegetable oil
  2 teaspoons salt
  ½ teaspoon sugar
  ¼ teaspoon monosodium glutamate

Wash the broccoli and cut the flowerets off the stems. Peel off the stringy outsides of the stems, then cut into 1-inch pieces. Drop stems and flowerets into boiling water for 2 minutes. Refresh immediately under cold water to stop the cooking. Drain.

Heat the oil in a skillet over a high heat. When hot, add the broccoli and stir until well covered with the oil. Mix in all remaining ingredients thoroughly. Add ¾ cup water, cover pan, reduce heat to medium and cook for 5 minutes. Then stir. Uncover, turn heat to high and cook until almost all the liquid has been absorbed. Serve immediately.

A sufficient amount to serve 12 with other accompaniments for dinner.

Note: Grace Zia Chu is the author of *The Pleasures of Chinese Cooking,* published by Simon and Schuster, of which Mr. Craig Claiborne, Food Editor of The New York Times, says, "There is probably no one who has done more to familiarize the public with the food of her homeland than Madame Chu. Her book, simply written and easily understood, will enrich the table on a vaster scale."

CHOCOLATE ROLL

         Vegetable oil
    1   package (6-ounce size) chocolate pieces
    1   tablespoon powdered instant coffee
    5   eggs, separated
    1   cup sugar
         Cocoa
    1   cup heavy cream
    1   teaspoon vanilla

Lightly oil, then line, a jelly-roll pan with wax paper. Oil the wax paper lightly. Set aside.

Combine the chocolate and coffee in the top of a small double boiler and melt over hot, not boiling, water. Meanwhile, beat the egg yolks with an electric beater or in an electric mixer until sticky. Then gradually beat in ½ *cup of the sugar* until the mixture is as heavy as mayonnaise.

Beat the whites with a clean, dry beater until they begin to form peaks, then gradually beat in the remaining sugar. Continue beating until you have a stiff, shiny meringue. Stir the melted chocolate into the yolk mixture thoroughly. Then beat in about a third of the meringue with a whisk. Fold in the remainder gently, but thoroughly, with a rubber spatula. Pour into the prepared pan, smoothing it gently so it reaches all sides.

Bake in a preheated 375° F. oven for 15 to 20 minutes or until the roll begins to shrink away from the sides of the pan. The baked roll will seem firm to the touch but that's the way it should be.

To remove from the pan, first run a knife down each side. Then, wring a dish towel out in cold water, cover the roll tightly and allow to cool. When cold, remove the cloth and dust generously with cocoa. Turn out onto a piece of wax paper longer than the length of the roll.

Whip the cream with a pinch of salt until thick, flavor with vanilla and spread on the roll. Roll up, using the paper to edge it along. Refrigerate.

Cut into 12 even pieces. Serve with *Chocolate Sauce:*

CHOCOLATE SAUCE

    1 cup white sugar
    1 cup light brown sugar, firmly packed
    2 squares (1-ounce size) unsweetened chocolate
    2 tablespoons butter
    1 cup water

Combine all the ingredients in the top of a double boiler. Place over moderate heat and stir until dissolved. To serve warm, place over boiling water. Otherwise, serve at room temperature. Makes about 3 cups.

ALMOND NUT ROLL

      Vegetable oil
    1 cup unblanched almonds, ground
    5 eggs, separated
    1 cup sugar
    1 teaspoon cinnamon
    3 tablespoons sifted confectioners' sugar
    1 cup heavy cream
    ½ teaspoon vanilla
      Pinch salt

Lightly oil, then line, a jelly-roll pan with wax paper. Lightly oil the paper. Set aside. Grind the almonds in an electric blender until very, very fine.

Beat the egg yolks with an electric beater or in an electric mixer, until thick, then gradually beat in ½ *cup of the sugar* and the cinnamon. Continue beating until the mixture is as thick as mayonnaise. Beat the egg whites with a clean, dry beater, until they just begin to take a shape. Gradually beat in the remaining sugar and continue beating until the meringue stands in stiff, shiny peaks.

Fold about ¼ *of the whites* into the yolk mixture, then a ¼ *cup of the ground nuts.* Continue, a fourth of each at a time, alternately, until all are used.

Pour into the prepared pan and spread to all sides gently with a spatula. Bake in a preheated 375° F. oven for 18 minutes or until the roll begins to shrink away from the sides of the pan. Take out of the oven and cool in the pan.

When cold, dust with confectioners' sugar. Turn out on wax paper, several inches longer than the cake. Whip the cream with the vanilla and a pinch of salt and spread over the cake. Roll up, using the paper to edge it along. Refrigerate. Cut into 12 pieces to serve.

VII

Menu Five

Fillet of Sole Mousse with Shrimp Sauce

Chicken Veronique

Cauliflower Ring with Carrots Vichy

Green Beans, Vinaigrette

Babas aux Pêches Flambé

Coffee

FILLET OF SOLE MOUSSE

    3 pounds fillet of sole
    ½ teaspoon freshly grated nutmeg
    6 slices firm white bread crumbled fine*
    3 cups light cream
    1 teaspoon salt
    ¼ teaspoon white pepper
    5 egg whites

Butter two 9-inch ring mold pans generously and set aside. Put the fish through the meat grinder using the finest blade, place in a large bowl and sprinkle with the nutmeg. Cover. Soak the bread crumbs in the cream, then combine with the fish, salt, and pepper. Mix well. Best done with your hands.

Beat the egg whites until they stand in firm, shiny peaks when the beater is held straight up. Whisk about a third into the fish mixture briskly, then fold in the remainder with a rubber spatula thoroughly, but gently. Spoon the mixture into the two molds, dividing it evenly. Cover each with buttered wax paper, butter side down, tie securely, and place in a large roasting pan, filling the pan to one-half the depth of the molds with boiling water.

Place in a preheated 375° F. oven and bake for 45 minutes. To serve, remove wax paper, run a knife around the edges carefully, then turn out onto hot platters. Serve with hot Shrimp Sauce. Serves 12.

* *Note:* Breadcrumbs are easy and quick to make in the electric blender.

SHRIMP SAUCE

    3 pounds green shrimp
    1 tablespoon vegetable oil
    3 tablespoons dry sherry
    4 tablespoons butter
    4 tablespoons flour
    ½ teaspoon salt
    3 cups milk, heated

Wash, shell and devein the shrimp. Reserve the shells. Heat the oil in a heavy skillet, add the shrimp and cook for 1 minute or until the shrimp have turned pink. Take out of the pan, place in a bowl, and combine with the sherry. Add the shrimp shells to the same skillet with the butter. Mash together, using a potato masher. Place over a medium heat and stir in the flour. When the mixture just begins to bubble, take off the heat, add the milk and salt, put back over a medium heat and bring to a boil, stirring constantly. Strain the sauce through a very fine sieve over the shrimp, pressing with a rubber spatula to extract all the sauce clinging to the shells. Discard shells. Pour the Shrimp Sauce into the top of a double boiler and keep hot, over hot water, until ready to serve.

To serve, pour half the Shrimp Sauce into the center of each mousse and garnish with bouquets of fresh watercress.

CHICKEN VÉRONIQUE

7 chicken breasts, skinned and boned (14 half breasts)
  Flour
1 pound white seedless grapes or 2 cans (8¾-ounce size)
¼ cup vegetable oil
2 peeled garlic cloves, slivered
4 tablespoons butter
2 tablespoons cornstarch
1 cup chicken stock, your own or canned condensed broth
1 teaspoon salt
  White pepper
½ cup dry white wine or dry vermouth

Dry the chicken breasts carefully and thoroughly with paper towels. Flour lightly, shaking off any excess. Wash and dry fresh grapes; drain canned ones.

Pour the oil into a large, heavy skillet, add the garlic and cook for 2 minutes taking care not to allow it to burn or it will turn bitter. Discard the garlic and add the butter. When hot, add the breasts—only as many as the pan can accommodate without crowding—and sauté 3 minutes on one side, then turn and sauté on the other side for 2 minutes. Press the tops with your fingers. They are springy to the touch when cooked perfectly. Lift out of the fat and set aside.

Mix the cornstarch with the chicken stock until smooth and stir into the pan. Add salt and pepper, place over a low heat and cook, stirring constantly with a wooden spoon, until the sauce thickens lightly. Stir in the grapes and wine, taste for seasoning, then add the chicken breasts. Bring up to a boil. Do not cook further.

Arrange the hot chicken breasts around the edge of a large, hot platter. Mound the grape sauce in the center and spoon the sauce coating over each breast. Serves 12.

Note: When breast of chicken is removed raw from one side of the bird, skinned and boned, it is known as a *suprême*. Each breast has two *suprêmes*.

CAULIFLOWER RING

     2 tablespoons butter
     ½ cup minced onion
     2 medium firm cauliflower
     ½ teaspoon salt
     ½ cup freshly grated Parmesan cheese
     ⅔ cup fresh bread crumbs [page oo]
     5 eggs, slightly beaten
     1 cup milk, heated

Butter two 9-inch ring mold pans well. Set aside.

Melt the remaining butter in a skillet and sauté the onion, [page 13].

Break the heads of cauliflower into flowerets. Wash and drop into a large kettle of rapidly boiling, salted water. Bring up to a boil again quickly. Reduce heat to moderate and cook, uncovered, for about 10 minutes or until a knife will pierce the stems easily. It's a good idea to taste. You do not want it overcooked. Drain. Then press through a fine sieve or mill to make a smooth purée. Measure 3 cups of the purée into a large bowl, add the cooked onion, salt, cheese, bread crumbs and eggs. Mix together thoroughly, adding the hot milk gradually. Spoon into the prepared molds. Place in a large pan, add enough boiling water to reach to about two-thirds of the mold. Bake in the lower part of a preheated 375° F. oven for 40 minutes. When a knife plunged in the center of the ring comes out dry, the ring is done. Turn out at once onto hot platters and keep warm.

While cauliflower rings bake, prepare the *Carrots Vichy:*

CARROTS VICHY

Scrape and wash 2 bunches young, tender carrots. Then slice, across, about ¼-inch thick. Drop into a kettle of boiling salted water. When water comes to a boil again, reduce heat to moderate and cook, covered, until just tender when pierced with the point of a small sharp knife. Or, better, taste for tenderness. Drain.

Melt 3 tablespoons of butter in the saucepan, return the carrots, add ½ cup finely chopped parsley sprigs and ½ cup sliced stuffed olives. Shake over a good heat until well mixed and piping hot. Spoon into center of Cauliflower Rings. Serve at once. Serves 12.

GREEN BEANS, VINAIGRETTE

Wash 3 pounds fresh, firm, young green beans. Remove strings, if any. Bring a very large kettle of several quarts of salted water to a rolling boil. When boiling, add a handful of the beans at a time so as not to stop the boiling. When water reaches a rolling boil a second time, reduce heat and cook slowly, uncovered, for 8 to 10 minutes or until *al dente*—crisp to the tongue. Drain immediately and refresh in cold water to stop the cooking, retain the color and crispness. When cold, drain thoroughly again and pat dry on a fresh clean towel.

If beans are to be served cold, they can be covered and refrigerated; if hot, they can be reheated in rapidly boiling, salted water and drained immediately or they can be tossed in hot butter over moderate heat until hot through. If heated, serve immediately.

SAUCE VINAIGRETTE FOR 12

½ teaspoon Dijon mustard (optional)
Salt
Freshly-ground pepper
¼ cup wine vinegar or lemon juice
½ cup French peanut oil or vegetable oil

Combine the mustard, salt and pepper to taste, and the vinegar. Beat with a whisk until well mixed and the salt has dissolved. Very gradually add the oil—correctly, drop by drop—whisking constantly. Taste here for seasoning. It may need more salt, pepper or even vinegar.

Chopped fresh herbs such as minced parsley, chives, tarragon or basil may be added or a pinch of dried herbs.

Toss the green beans in the dressing just before serving. Allow about 1 tablespoon of dressing per person or just enough to coat the greens lightly.

BABAS AUX PÊCHES

3 tablespoons butter
1 cup all-purpose flour
1 cake compressed or active-dry yeast
3 eggs
3 tablespoons sugar
  Pinch salt

Butter 12 baba pans thoroughly and set aside.

Sprinkle the yeast over ¼ cup lukewarm water to soften; place the flour in a warm bowl (rinsed in hot water, then dried). Add the softened yeast and eggs to the flour and beat lightly with your hand until well blended. Cover with a fresh towel and set in a warm place, away from drafts, until the dough doubles in bulk. About ¾ of an hour.

Meanwhile, work 2 *tablespoons of the butter* until soft with your hands, then work in the sugar and salt. When the dough has risen sufficiently, punch down and mix in the butter-sugar combination. Fill the prepared pans half full, cover again with a clean towel, and allow to rise in a warm place, away from drafts, until *almost* double in bulk. Bake in a preheated 450° F. oven for 12 to 14 minutes or until golden. Turn out at once and place in a flat dish.

Meanwhile, make this syrup: Combine ¾ cup of sugar with ¾ cup of the peach juice from canned Freestone peaches and 2 tablespoons of dark rum or Southern Comfort. Cook over a moderate heat until it has thickened lightly. Pour immediately over the cooked babas while they are still hot. Spoon any syrup that runs into the dish over the babas as you think of it.

To serve, place each baba on a peach half, arrange on a round, silver platter. Heat 3 tablespoons of Southern Comfort, ignite and pour over all the Babas.

A GLOSSARY FOR THE NEW BRIDE

---

3 Saucepans—1-qt., 2-qt., and 3-qt.—with covers
1 10-qt. Soup Pot with two side handles
1 6-inch Fry Pan with lid
1 12-inch Fry Pan with lid
1 10-inch Omelette Pan, 1 8-inch Omelette Pan
1 Dutch Oven
1 Kettle
2 Coffee Makers—2-cup and 8-cup
1 Griddle
1 Bread Box
1 Canister set with lids

And for your oven . . .

PIE PAN

Most recipes call for 8- and 9-inch pans.

CAKE PANS

You should have both square and round, again in 8- or 9-inch sizes.

COVERED CASSEROLES

For one-dish meals that can go right to the table. Convenient sizes have 2- or 3-quart capacity. These are available with serving caddies or warming stands.

ROASTING PAN

It should be at least 12 x 9 inches for small roasts or chickens, with a rack.

COOKIE SHEETS

You should have two. They're not only ideal for baking cookies, but handy for heating frozen foods such as pies, french fries and pizzas.

MUFFIN PAN

Particularly handy when non-stick coated, these are a must for cupcakes, rolls, biscuits, popovers and muffins, and can also be used for cooking individual dishes like croquettes.

A set of four measuring cups, graduated from ¼ cup to 1 cup.

A graduated measuring cup for hot or cold liquids.

A set of measuring spoons. (Did you know it takes 3 teaspoonfuls to equal 1 tablespoon?)

A juicer.

A rotary beater.

A set of implements including a long-handled fork, a large basting spoon, narrow spatula, pancake turner, soup ladle, slotted spoon and two or three mixing spoons.

Small- and medium-size strainers and a large colander.

A set of round biscuit cutters.

A set of mixing bowls.

Assorted knives for paring, slicing vegetables and carving, and scissors.

A can opener and at least two bottle-top openers.

An Oster blender.

A set of wooden spoons.

A pyrex set of bowls—small.

2 Rubbermaid spatulas.

6 dish towels.

6 glass towels.

4 pot holders.